Historical Atlases of South Asia,
Central Asia, and the Middle East

A HISTORICAL ATLAS OF

PAKISTAN

Robert Greenberger

The Rosen Publishing Group, Inc.

For all those who want to live in peace

Published in 2003 by The Rosen Publishing Group, Inc.
29 East 21st Street, New York, NY 10010

Library of Congress Cataloging-in-Publication Data

Greenberger, Robert.
A Historical Atlas of Pakistan / Robert Greenberger. — 1st ed.
p. cm. — (Historical atlases of South Asia, Central Asia, and the Middle East)
Includes bibliographical references and index.
ISBN 0-8239-3866-2
1. Pakistan — History — Juvenile literature. I. Title. II. Series.
DS382 .G74 2002
954.91 — dc21

2002031715

Manufactured in the United States of America

Cover image: Newly reelected president Pervez Musharraf *(upper left)*, the Mughal tomb of medieval emperor Akbar *(bottom left)*, and Gulab Singh of Jammu, founder of the last ruling house of Kashmir, *(right)* are pictured atop a modern and a historical map of Pakistan.

Contents

NORTHERN
AREAS

NORTH-WEST
FRONTIER
PROVINCE

KĀBUL

Peshawar

TRIBAL AREAS

ISLAMABAD

Gum

PUNJAB

Kandahār

Quetta

Indus

BALUCHISTAN

Kap Salt Swamp

SINDH

Dash

Indu

Na

Karachi

Mouth of the Indus

ARABIAN SEA

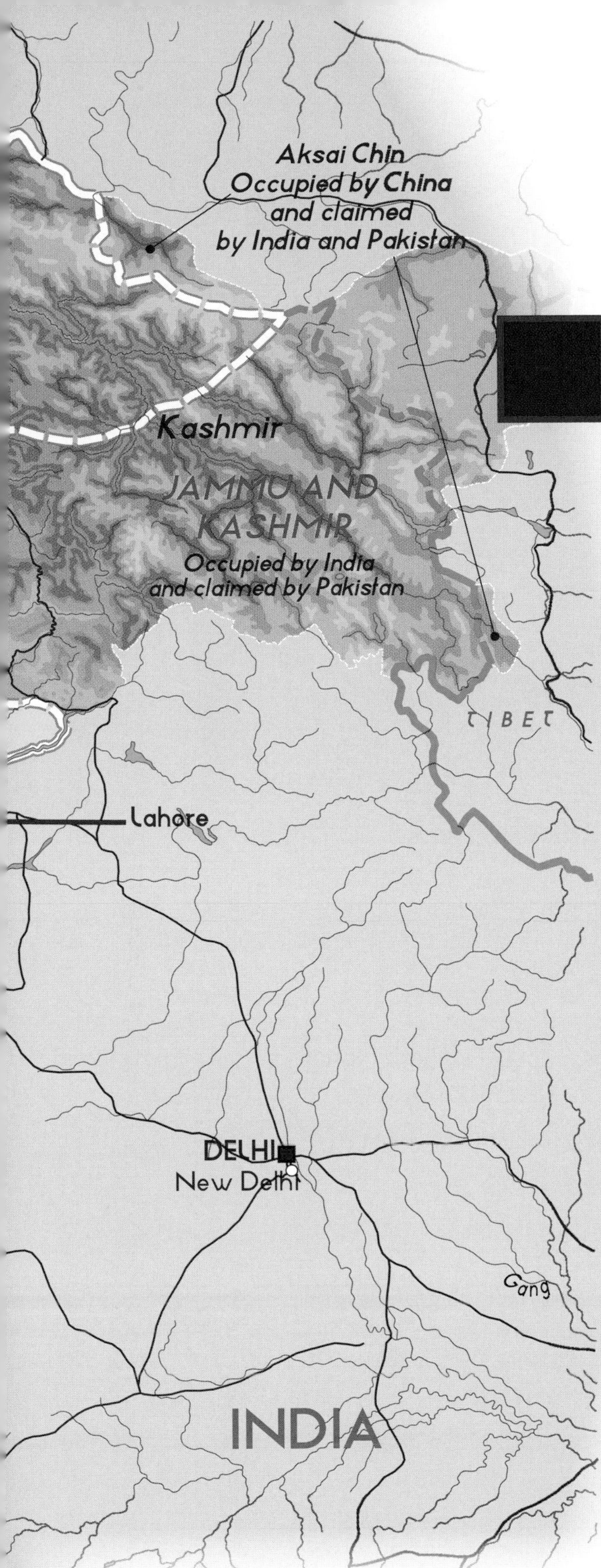

INTRODUCTION

Pakistan, like India, was once a part of the Indus Valley civilization (3000–1500 BC), one of the oldest civilizations in the world. Though the ancient community was largely situated around the Indus River, its total reach was much farther. It extended from Afghanistan to northern India in the north, and from the Iranian border to Bombay (present-day Mumbai), India, in the south. Much evidence remains from this period, such as ancient pottery, tools, the ruins of carefully planned towns, and one of the oldest surviving burial grounds. Pakistan's most famous Indus archaeological sites are called Harappa and Mohenjo-Daro. Harappa is located in Pakistan's Punjab province on its eastern border, and Mohenjo-Daro ("The Mound of the Dead") is found in the Sindh province.

Pakistan, once a part of British India, separated to form a Muslim country in 1947. At first, it separated into two sections—West Pakistan and East Pakistan. East Pakistan later became the formally recognized nation of Bangladesh in 1971. Present-day Pakistan still faces various conflicts with neighboring India over Jammu and Kashmir, northern territories of which both countries claim ownership.

Aksai Chin
Occupied by China
and claimed
by India and Pakistan

Kashmir

JAMMU AND KASHMIR
Occupied by India
and claimed by Pakistan

TIBET

Lahore

DELHI
New Delhi

Gang

INDIA

Today, Pakistan shares its borders with Iran, Afghanistan, China, and India. It has 310,300 square miles (803,940 sq. km) of land borders.

From the dawn of time until Pakistan was granted its independence in 1947, Pakistanis rarely lived as they desired. Instead, the region that now contains the nation known as Pakistan was overrun by other cultures. Its people were often forced to embrace foreign leaders.

South Asia has remained volatile and unstable since its independence from the British. This instability has prevented its prosperity. Pakistan's and India's lands were conquered many times, which introduced various languages and other cultural attributes into both countries. Like every Asian country, Pakistan has a long, rich history marked by invasion and conquest. It is also a place where the world's greatest religions, such as Hinduism and Islam, prospered.

Even today, the people of Pakistan remain unsettled. The nation's current tension is largely due to the ethnic conflict between people who migrated to Pakistan after 1947—*muhajirs*—and those local people—Punjabis and Sindhis—who were already living there. Both groups do not allow acceptance of each other, so their disagreements have been the cause

The ancient site of Mohenjo-Daro, where this sculpture of a high priest was unearthed in the 1920s, was a city carefully planned and constructed on a grid. Its population most likely worshiped many gods and goddesses as well as animals.

of much of the region's tensions. Still another major problem is rivalry between the Sunni and Shiite Muslims.

When Pakistan finally received independence from British-controlled India, the Muslims gained their own country. However, the separation of the land left disputed areas, known as Jammu and Kashmir, claimed by both Indians and Pakistanis. Today, they continue to argue over the ownership of this mountainous territory, leaving its borders undefined.

1 A CRADLE OF CIVILIZATION

Some of the earliest evidence of man's development can be traced to Pakistan. In the Indus Valley, remains from the Stone Age continue to be found. The Indus Valley civilization, or the Harappan civilization as it is sometimes referred to, can be dated to some 5,000 years ago. Nomadic tribes were located in the Soan Valley of the Potwar Plateau, in the eastern Punjab province that borders India. From as far back as 4000 BC, there is proof of agriculture and, less than 1,000 years later, permanent settlements. Being a valley, its fertile conditions allowed humans to sustain themselves and prosper. Support from the fertile lands encouraged once nomadic tribes to settle. Archaeologists have found remains of settlements around present-day Baluchistan, a southwest region of Pakistan enclosed by Afghanistan, Iran, and the Arabian Sea. The people who lived there raised animals and grew crops such as barley. Sometime between the first and second millennia, these clusters became cities. People engaged in trade across the Arabian Sea with other flourishing civilizations, such as Mesopotamia.

Ancient Cultures

Archaeological excavations determined that these ancient people forged their own tools, usually using copper and bronze, and jewelry, using gold and silver.

They also formed clay into pottery and wove cotton into textiles, as recent archaeological evidence suggests.

An archaeological dig at Kot Diji, a location in the Sindh province, provided experts with more information. Archaeologists were able to date the culture to 3000 BC. Kot Diji is now considered one of the earliest urban communities, having prospered from 2500 to 1800 BC. Evidence points to many forms of sophisticated art, as well as a drainage system, public baths, and brick structures. These people formed their own written pictographic language, known as either Mohenjodaran or Harappan. To this day, it eludes translation.

At much the same time that the civilization of Kot Diji disappeared, the rest of present-day India was being settled by various nomadic tribes. These people rode horses from the north and west, farmed the land, and tended cattle.

The Vedic Civilization

Historians and archaeologists now believe that the Punjab region was invaded around 1800 BC. They believe that Aryans, a seminomadic people, migrated from Central Asia through the Hindu Kush. This is a mountain chain that follows the northern Pakistan border with both present-day Tajikistan and Afghanistan. These people rode horses, raised cattle, and established one of the world's first languages, an early form of Sanskrit. The evidence of this language can now be seen in

ASIA MINOR

MEDITERRANEAN SEA

Memphis

Nile

Early civilizations located in what is now Pakistan constructed sophisticated cities. The people developed their own pictographic language and built forts, protective walls, and drainage systems as early as 2500 BC. The site of the Kot Diji fort (right), located 25 miles (40 kilometers) east of Mohenjo-Daro, proved to scholars that Pakistan's history was even older than previously believed. The fort predates Mohenjo-Daro and Harappa by at least 500 years.

CASPIAN
SEA

Tigris

Nineveh

Euphrates

Susa

Babylon

Persepolis

Ur

ARABIAN DESERT

PERSIAN GULF

RED SEA

CASPIAN SEA

PERSIAN EMPIRE

Euphrates

Tigris

○ Babylon

○ Susa

Persian Gulf

Indus

ARABIAN SEA

INDIAN OCEAN

Though not as widely practiced today, ancient religions such as Zoroastrianism and Buddhism continue to have a following. People who practice Zoroastrianism (known today as Parsees) know the religion from the Persian prophet Zoroaster (638–553 BC). After his death, nomads carried his teachings throughout the Persian Empire. Buddhism, like Zoroastrianism, originated from one man—Siddharta Gautama Buddha (586–483 BC). Buddhism spread throughout India and Asia in the sixth century BC. The fragment of a frieze (*bottom left*) represents Buddha and dates from the Gandharan period. It was discovered in Taxila.

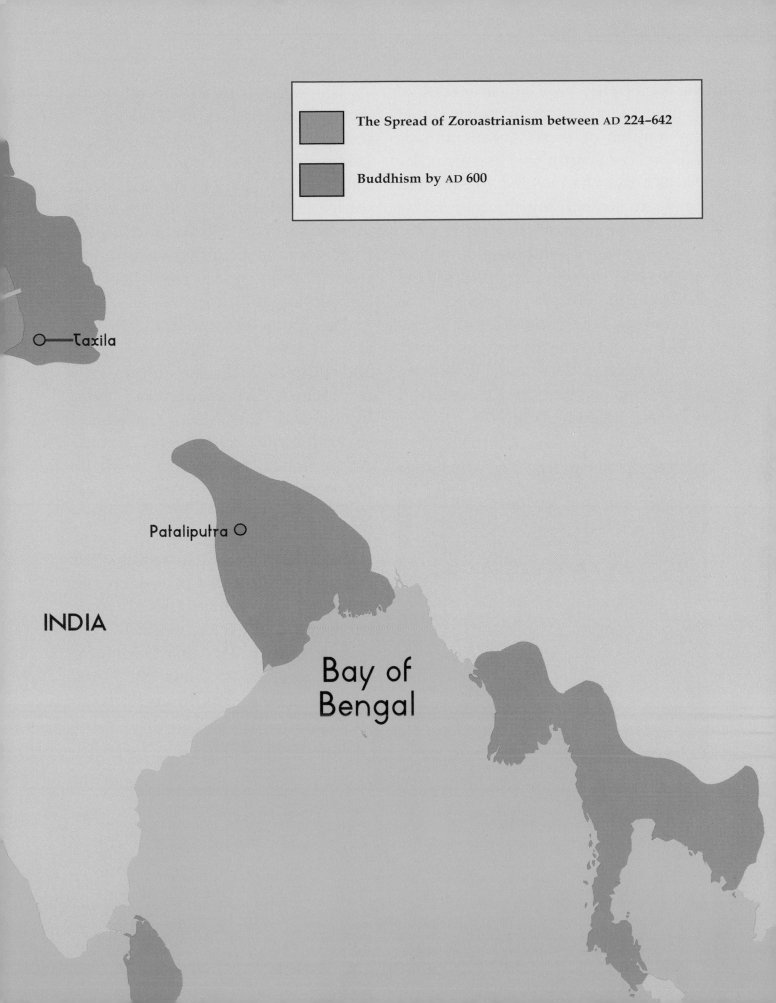

The Spread of Zoroastrianism between AD 224–642

Buddhism by AD 600

O——Taxila

Pataliputra O

INDIA

Bay of
Bengal

the ancient *Rig Veda*, an early book of hymns. Archaeologists believe that the religion of these Aryan nomads was an early form of Hinduism. By 900 BC, they had settled in northern Pakistan, establishing the foundation of the Vedic civilization.

There was no centralized kingdom at the time. Smaller communities, the largest of which covered the Peshawar, Lower Swat, and Kabul Valleys, and was known as Gandhara, emerged. Eventually, Gandhara established capitals in Pushkalavati (Charsadda) and Taxila.

The entire Indus Plain fell to the Achaemenid rulers of Iran, who at the time of their leadership established the largest empire the world had ever known. Cyrus the Great, the leader of that empire, crossed the Hindu Kush in 530 BC and, in less than a decade, Gandhara became the twelfth satrapy (territory) of the Achaemenian Empire.

Persepolis became the site of a grand palace for Achaemenid rulers, and, little by little, the empire grew to include Mesopotamia, Syria, Egypt, and Asia Minor, as well as several Greek cities and islands. Achaemenid rulers practiced the Zoroastrian faith and carefully controlled their large territory with a variety of overseers.

Buddha began his teachings during the sixth century BC, which later spread throughout the south Asian subcontinent. It was toward the end of this century, too, that Darius I of Persia, the son of Cyrus the Great, organized the Sindh and Punjab lands as the twentieth satrapy of the Achaemenian Empire.

The inscription on this monument once graced the tomb of Cyrus the Great, founder of the Persian Empire. It begins simply, "I am Cyrus, King and Achaemenid."

A LAND CONSTANTLY CONQUERED

The Persians ruled the entire empire until, under Darius III, it fell to Alexander the Great, a Macedonian warrior, in 330 BC. He arrived in the Indus region in 327 BC only to have his army mutiny two years later. Alexander established several Macedonian settlements in Punjab. Thousands of ships carried his soldiers home after the mutiny via the Persian Gulf. Others remained to help govern the area.

After Alexander's death, one of his soldiers, a general named Seleucus, established a dynasty composed of Persia, Afghanistan, and Gandhara. It was not peaceful; Chandragupta Maurya, leader of the Mauryan Empire, which was based in what is now India's Lower Ganges Basin, attacked Seleucus in 305 BC. The clash led to a series of battles that later subsided. Eventually, Maurya and Seleucus became friends. Seleucus allowed Maurya to take Greek settlements in the northwest in return for peace. Legend tells that the price was 500 elephants.

From 269 to 232 BC, Asoka, grandson of Chandragupta, ruled the Mauryan Empire in an unprecedented era of artistic greatness. He concentrated his territory in what is now northeast India and the northern Punjab region of Pakistan. He established the ancient city of Taxila as a center of religion and learning. Asoka was also one of the first rulers to practice Buddhism,

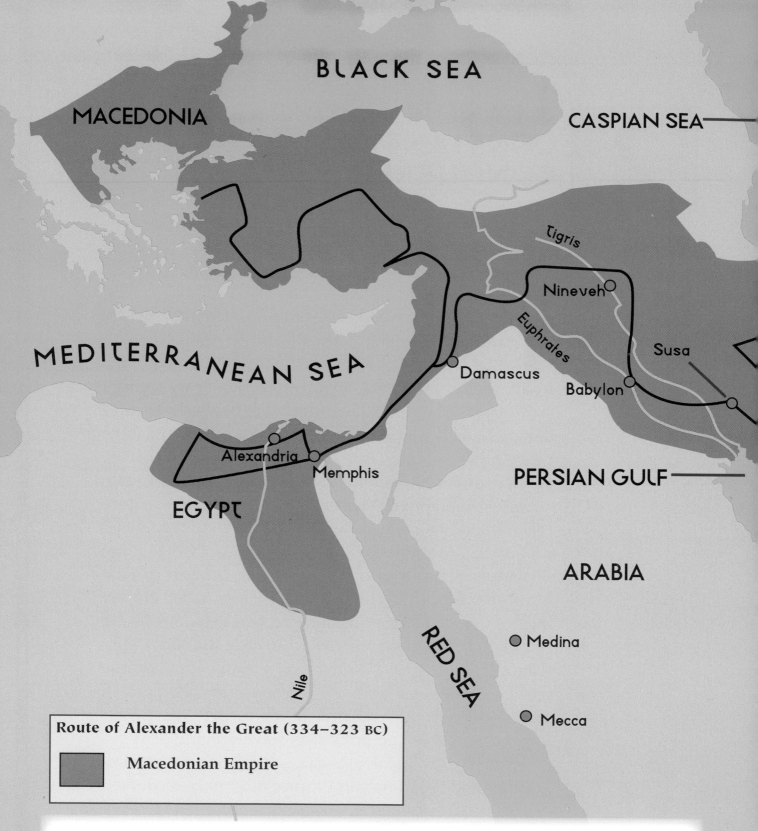

Route of Alexander the Great (334–323 BC)

Macedonian Empire

BLACK SEA

MACEDONIA

CASPIAN SEA

Tigris

Nineveh

MEDITERRANEAN SEA

Euphrates

Susa

Damascus

Babylon

Alexandria

Memphis

PERSIAN GULF

EGYPT

ARABIA

Medina

Nile

RED SEA

Mecca

Alexander the Great (*top right*, 356–323 BC), who remains one of history's most accomplished military leaders, inherited his ambitions to overtake Asia after his father was murdered in 336 BC. During Alexander's conquests, he founded seventeen cities throughout present-day Afghanistan, Iran, and Egypt, which all bore his name. More than anything, Alexander the Great wanted the sophisticated culture of Asia to mix with his own Greek ancestry.

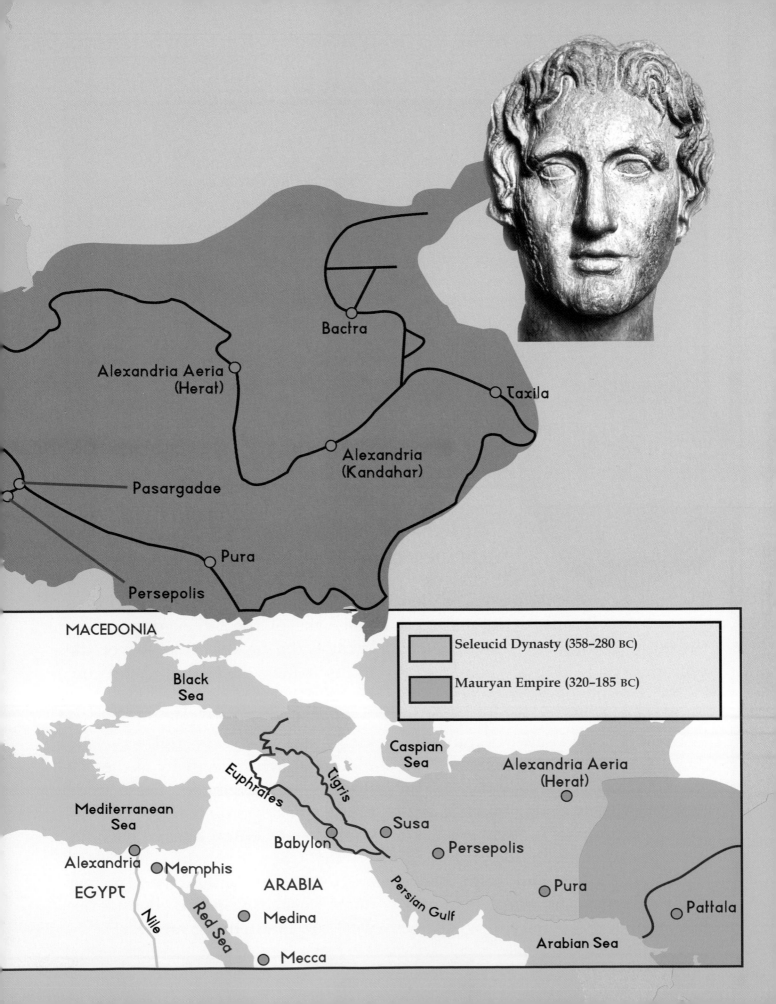

Bactra

Alexandria Aeria
(Herat)

Taxila

Alexandria
(Kandahar)

Pasargadae

Pura

Persepolis

MACEDONIA

Black
Sea

Seleucid Dynasty (358–280 BC)

Mauryan Empire (320–185 BC)

Caspian
Sea

Alexandria Aeria
(Herat)

Euphrates

Tigris

Mediterranean
Sea

Susa

Babylon

Persepolis

Alexandria

Memphis

Pura

EGYPT

ARABIA

Persian Gulf

Pattala

Nile

Red Sea

Medina

Arabian Sea

Mecca

Gandharan Art

Under Asoka, people expressed themselves artistically. This period, stretching from the first until the seventh century AD, left behind numerous paintings, sculptures, and pottery, all devoted to Buddhist works. This period is also responsible for the first works that represented the Buddha in human form. This style of Buddhist-inspired art developed in the region now known as Pakistan and Afghanistan, and was highly influenced by Greek and Roman art and sculpture, which flourished 500 years earlier. In fact, Gandharan art is often referred to as the Graeco- or Roman-Buddhist school, and the influence of the Greeks can often be recognized in certain Gandharan motifs, such as vine scrolls and cherubs bearing garlands. The tile *(left)*, for example, which dates from the period, appears decidedly Greek or Hellenistic. After Asoka's death, other rulers patronized the arts, too, including Kanishka. Under Kanishka, the Silk Road between Peshawar and the Indus Valley flourished, securing the commercial and cultural prosperity of the entire region.

which had begun to establish itself 300 years earlier.

Buddhism later spread throughout the entire lower Asian region.

As a result of his conversion to Buddhism, Asoka spoke against violence and issued laws of morality. Some of his lessons, inscribed on stone tablets, survive today as an example of his enlightened leadership. Unfortunately, this era died with Asoka, though the Gandhara region adapted to Buddhism thanks to his influence. The Mauryan Empire had dwindled by 180 BC, when the last ruler was killed. The region then splintered into smaller territories.

Meanwhile, Bactrians, rulers of the Afghan and Persian regions in the wake of the Greek occupation, became the newest rulers over the Indus Valley, including Gandhara, by 100 BC.

However, during this time, other kingdoms rose and fell as trade routes, known collectively as the Silk Road, were developed. These trade routes began to connect Rome, Greece, and Central Asia with China. As the Chinese pushed westward and the various Middle Eastern kingdoms pushed eastward, boundaries were constantly being revised.

The Gandhara region was, at various times, ruled by the Indo-Greek king Menander (who ruled from 155 to 130 BC), the Scythians, who conquered most of the Indian region, and the Parthians. Given the location of trade routes and waterways, the Gandhara region was among the most frequently conquered.

By the second century, the Kushanas (AD 78–200) had conquered the region. King Kanishka cultivated Buddhism, which first flourished in Gandhara, and the religion was absorbed into daily life. Gandhara was transformed into a center of religious study and artistic expression. It was also in Gandhara that advanced learning first developed, and one of the greatest universities in the ancient world was established.

The Gupta Dynasty

After Kanishka's reign, though, the Kushan Empire crumbled. Gandhara and Kashmir were claimed by the Sassanid rulers of Persia. Other portions of the empire, including eastern Punjab, were absorbed by the Gupta dynasty, which ruled most of

This capital of a pillar, which dates from the reign of Asoka (273–232 BC), was once one of many 32-foot (10-meter) high sandstone columns that were erected to commemorate events in Buddha's life as well as mark holy Buddhist sites. Its lions symbolize Buddha's teachings to the four corners of the world. The wheels below them are called the Dharma Chakra, or Wheels of Law.

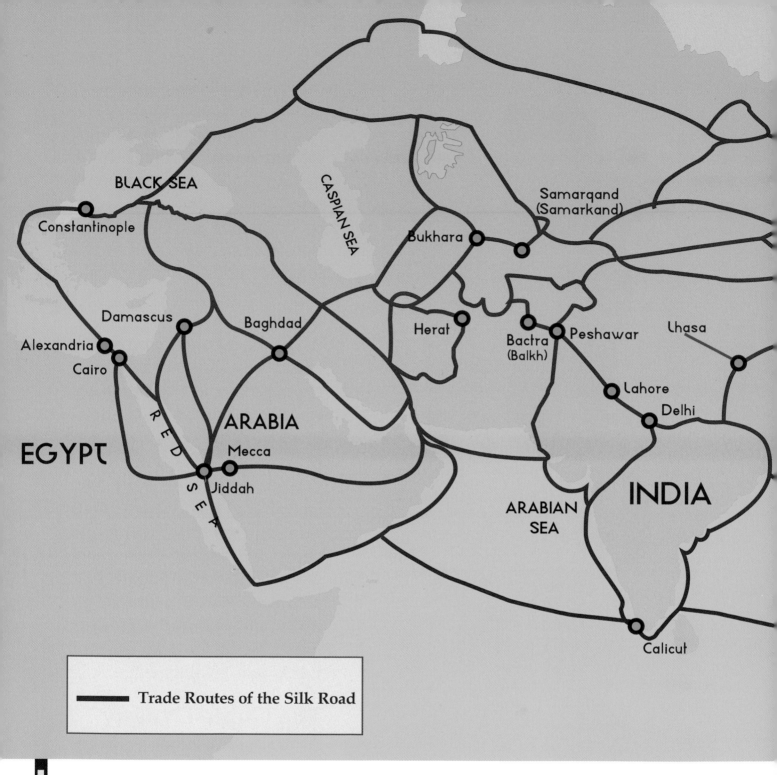

The Silk Road—some 5,000 miles (8,047 kilometers) of trade routes over land and sea—emerged around 100 BC. For centuries, the ancient trade routes served merchants traveling from the Mediterranean to Asia and helped introduce Europe to many desirable items, including exotic foods, spices, ivory, jade, precious stones, and, of course, legendary Asian silks. Later, around AD 600, during the rise and spread of Islam, Muslims dominated the ancient routes.

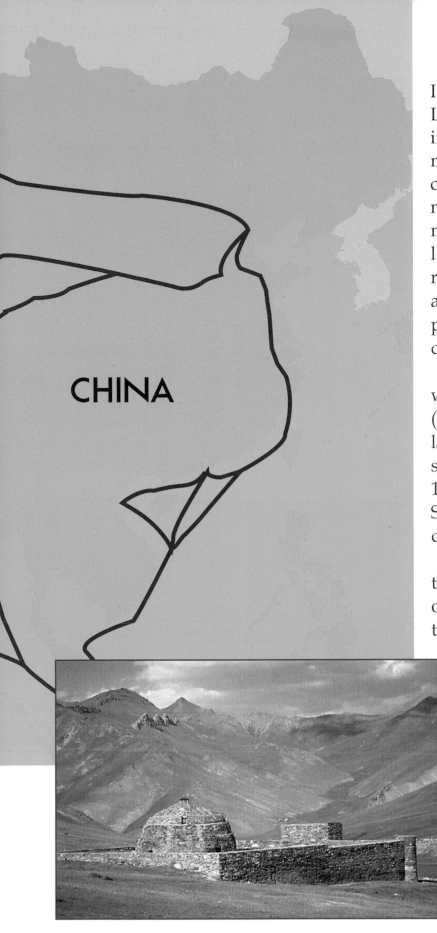

CHINA

India in the third century. Learning was cherished during the Gupta dynasty. Mathematicians developed several concepts such as zero and the numerical symbols. Astronomers studied the skies and learned that the world was round long before Europeans accepted the concept. Doctors performed operations and designed instruments.

Gandhara's golden age ended when the fierce Hephthalites (White Huns) raced across their land from Central Asia. Their stay was brief, probably less than 100 years. Afterward, the Turkic Shahi dynasty from Afghanistan drove them from Gandhara.

The Turkic Shahi remained the governing force throughout the ninth century, before the Hindu Shahi dynasty took control. This kingdom spanned more than 100 years and encompassed territories from Kabul Valley to Multan. In this new configuration, Hinduism spread farther into Asia.

3 THE COMING OF ISLAM

BLACK SEA

Alexandria——O

EGYPT

A new religion emerged in Mecca in the seventh century. An Arab merchant, Muhammad, preached Islam, ending age-old traditions of idol worship. By the time of Muhammad's death, Islam had spread across the Arabian Peninsula, and by the end of the seventh century, it had encompassed most of the Middle East and Persia (Iran). However, in AD 709, pirates seized an Arab ship off the Sindh coast. Seeking revenge, teenage warriors led by Muhammad bin Qasim returned two years later and sacked several Sindh villages. At the same time, Arab armies arrived over land. Suddenly, a new culture was introduced into the region.

By 724, Sindh was under Arab rule, setting the stage for change. Many Hindus converted to Islam, believing it was a faith that

Islam, which means "Submission to God," spread rapidly after the death of its prophet, Muhammad, in AD 632. The Muslim warning to nonbelievers was "[Accept] the Koran, [or pay] tribute [taxes], or [die by] the sword." For many, the transition to Islam was by force, but others welcomed the religion because it meant that they no longer had to pay tribute (taxes). In India, many Hindus and Buddhists were also converted by force, though some willingly changed their beliefs since Islam recognized the equality of man and denounced the caste system.

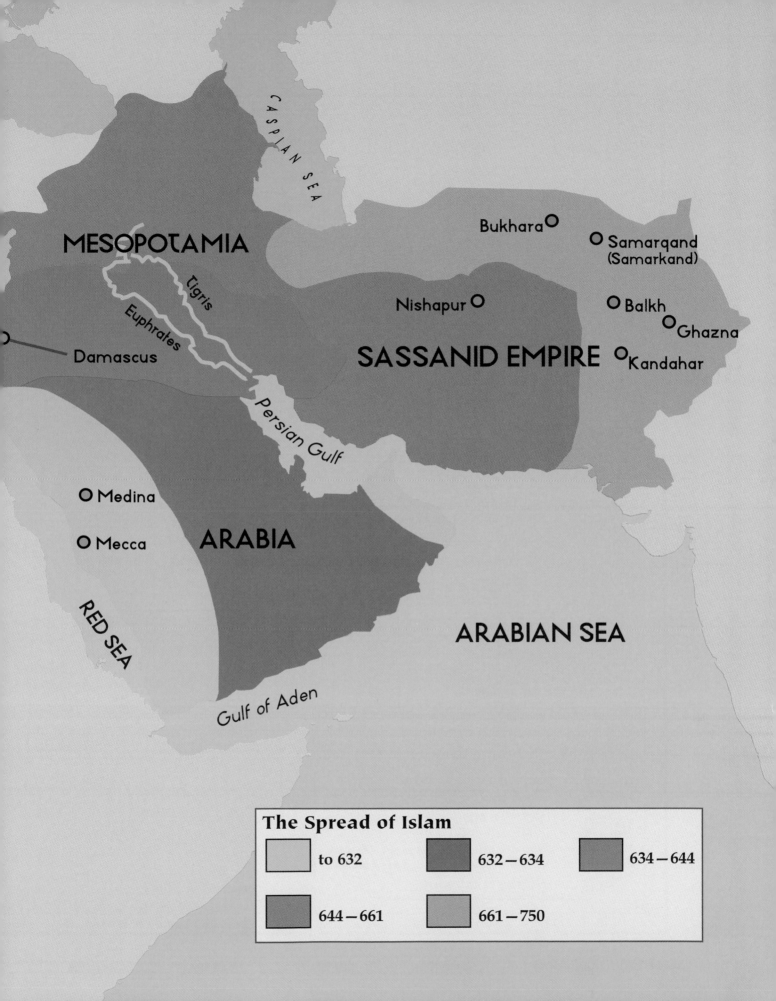

CASPIAN SEA

MESOPOTAMIA

Tigris

Euphrates

Damascus

Bukhara ○

○ Samarqand
(Samarkand)

Nishapur ○

○ Balkh

Ghazna

SASSANID EMPIRE

○ Kandahar

Persian Gulf

○ Medina

○ Mecca

ARABIA

ARABIAN SEA

RED SEA

Gulf of Aden

The Spread of Islam

to 632		632–634		634–644	
644–661		661–750			

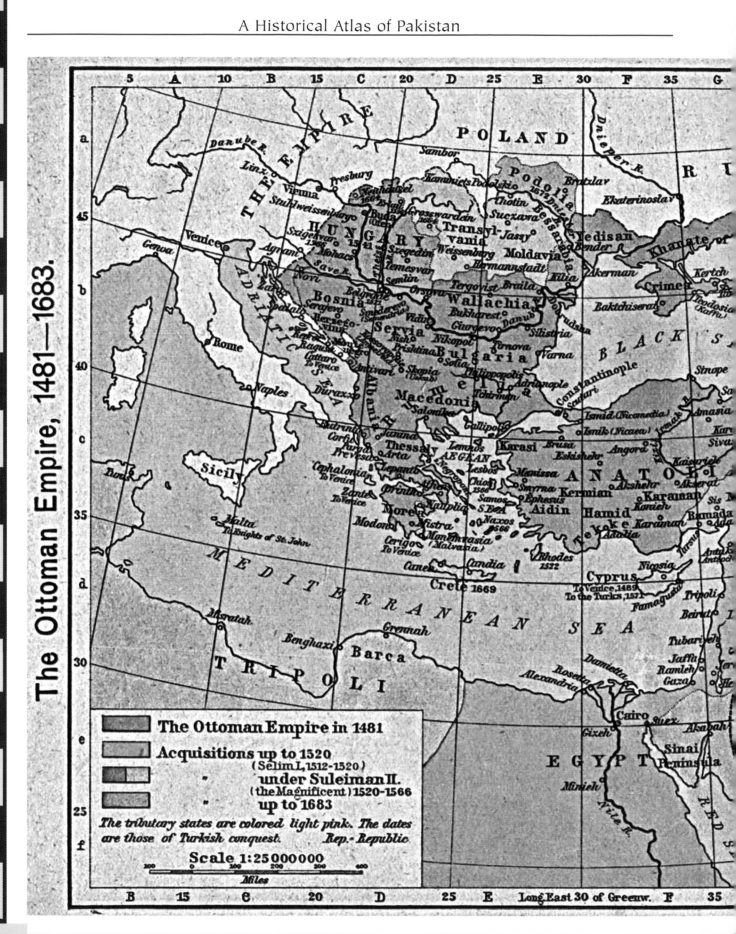

The Ottoman Empire, 1481—1683.

The Ottoman Empire in 1481
Acquisitions up to 1520
(Selim I, 1512-1520)
   "   **under Suleiman II.**
(the Magnificent) 1520-1566
   "   **up to 1683**

The tributary states are colored light pink. The dates are those of Turkish conquest.   Rep.- Republic.

Scale 1:25 000 000

Miles

would deliver them from the inequality of the caste system—a strict class division—and increase their social status. While under Muslim control, Sindh briefly became a part of the larger Muslim Empire—stretching from Spain to Persia—ruled by the caliph (spiritual leader) in Baghdad. The Muslim ruler in Sindh gave allegiance to the caliph, who allowed him to govern on his behalf. While Islam found believers among the people, most retained their previous beliefs. A significant Muslim presence in India would come later in the tenth century.

The Turks

The Ghaznavids, Turks who had settled in what is now Afghanistan, controlled the region from 977 to 1148. Military campaigns, led by Mahmud of Ghazni, extended the Ghaznavid Empire from present-day Iraq to India's Ganges River and from Khwarezm to the Arabian Sea. Muhammad Ghuri overthrew the Ghaznavid hold in 1148 and began twenty-five years of raids on Hindu cities, looting temples. The populace was forced to convert to a new religion. Whatever stability existed was ended when Muhammad Ghuri attacked Peshawar and Lahore, moving on to Delhi by 1193. After Ghuri's assassination, his general, Qutb-ud-Din Aybak, declared himself ruler. He established the Delhi sultanate, or Slave dynasty.

The Delhi sultanate was the first true Turk/Muslim kingdom in the region. Under

Although Muslims had acquired a huge empire since the spread of Islam began in the 600s, they had colonized little of it. By the eleventh century, Seljuq Turks had begun overtaking their empire in Ghazni, or present-day Afghanistan. Civil wars and tribal infighting also led to the disruption of Muslim strength and control.

This fourteenth-century detail of an Arabic manuscript, "The Arrival of an Indian Embassy Before Sultan Mahmud of Ghazni," was created by Raschid-el-Din. By this time, the Ghaznavid Empire had been weakened by Mongol hordes led by Genghis Khan and his predecessors.

Aybak and his successor, Iltimush, the sultanate expanded. It now covered most of northern India. India's first known female ruler, Raziya Sultan (Iltimush's daughter) also belonged to this dynasty. Genghis Khan and his Mongol hordes arrived in the region just over a century later, armies that left vast areas completely destroyed and thousands dead.

The Mughal Period

Over the next few centuries (from the 1200s), the Indus Valley region witnessed repeated invasions by Central Asian tribes such as the Mongols and Turks. These invasions continued the deterioration caused years before. This turmoil was compounded by the destruction ordered by another conqueror, Timur (Tamerlane). Timur was a Turk from Samarkand who had already been ravaging Delhi in invasions since 1398.

However, the northern India Delhi sultanate remained stable. During some periods, the sultan's

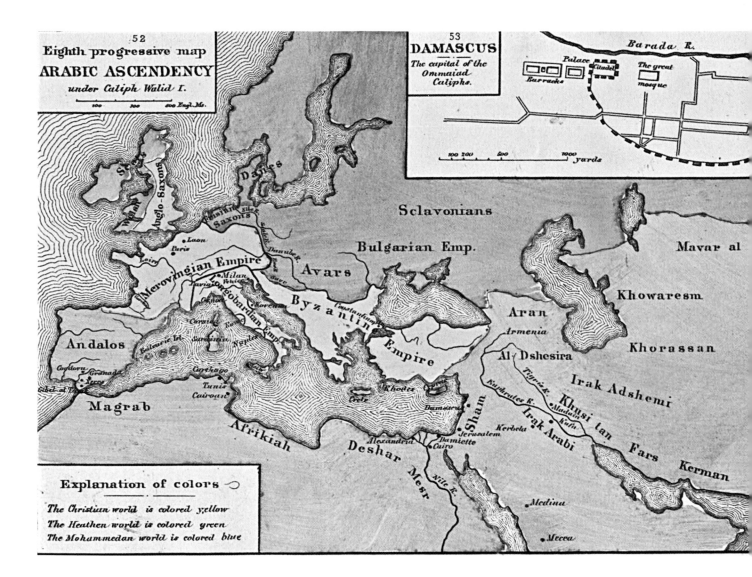

In the European medieval world, luxuries were rare, while the Muslim Empire gave birth to glamorous, well-lighted cities such as Baghdad and Damascus, education for many of its citizens, and the most modern medical care of the day, as well as plentiful universities and extensive libraries. Most scholarly writing of the period was written in Arabic, and Arabs ushered in the first sciences of anatomy, chemistry (then alchemy), and algebra. They also invented the astrolabe.

influence extended into the region now known as Pakistan. Under these Muslim monarchs based in Delhi, Islam gained influence. The religion was embraced in northern India, the Indus Valley, and later in south India and Bengal.

Through a succession of Muslim monarchs, Islam spread throughout the countryside, reaching people living in the northern mountains two centuries later. By the thirteenth century, Islam had settled into southern and western India. Accepting Islam meant accepting new cultural mores and expressions.

In the fifteenth century, Zahir-ud-din Muhammad Babur—"the Tiger"—a descendent of both Mongol emperors Genghis Khan and Timur,

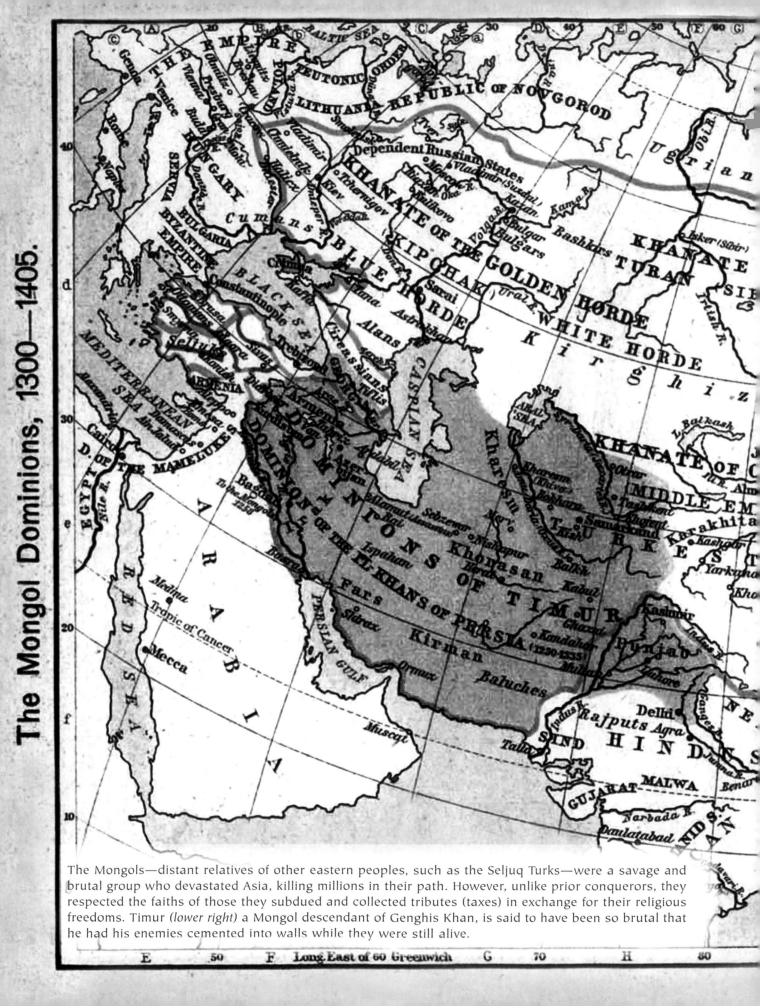

The Mongols—distant relatives of other eastern peoples, such as the Seljuq Turks—were a savage and brutal group who devastated Asia, killing millions in their path. However, unlike prior conquerors, they respected the faiths of those they subdued and collected tributes (taxes) in exchange for their religious freedoms. Timur (*lower right*) a Mongol descendant of Genghis Khan, is said to have been so brutal that he had his enemies cemented into walls while they were still alive.

Arctic Circle

moyedes

T u n g u s e s

Lena R.

Angara R.

Yenisei R.

Amur R.

Shilka R.

Argun R.

Onon R.

Amur R.

Sungari

Niuche

Manchus

Selenga R.

Orkon R.

Kerulen R.

Baikal L.

ai m a n s

Keraits

Karakorum

Khalkas

M O N G O L I A

K H A N

Khitans

Khambalig

(Peking)

Shangtu

Desert of Gobi

T H E   G R E A T

AI

k (Urumtsi) Khamil
(Hami)

gurs

Lop-nor

Yu-mon-kwan
(Kia-yu-kwan)

Kan-chau-fu

T A N G U T

Koko-nor

Taiyuen-fu

C A T H A Y

Hoang-ho

Kai-fong-fu

Great Wall

Great Canal

KOREA

JAPAN SEA

YELLOW SEA

NANGU. (JAPAN.)

ET

Si-ngan-fu

C H I N A

Cheng-tu-fu

Yang-tse-kiang

M A N Z I

Nanking

Zaitun
(Tsiun-chau-fu)

Lhasa

hmaputra R.

N ASSAM

Gaŭr

Irrawadi R.

Salwen R.

BURMA
Ava
Pagan

Si-kiang

Si-kiang

Mekong R.

TONG-KING

Kesho
(Hanoi)

Hai-nan

YUN-NAN

COCHIN-CHINA

BAY

OF

NGAL

PEGU

S I A M

CAMBODIA

Approximate limits of the Mongol
dominions about 1300
Approximate extent of the dominions
of Timur in 1405
Possessions of the Ottoman Turks
before } the battle of Angora (1402)
after }
D.- Dominion K.- Kingdom S.- Sultanate
Scale 1:48 000 000

200   0   200   400   600   800
Miles

fled his home in Mughalistan, in central Asia. Within the next few years, Babur conquered the territories of present-day Afghanistan and Pakistan, and defeated the sultan of Delhi in a decisive battle in 1528. In doing so, he established the Mughal dynasty, which ruled most of the Indian subcontinent for the next three centuries.

The Mughal dynasty, however, suffered an early setback when

Mughal India experienced a gardening renaissance of sorts, with emperors such as Babur, seen here on a page from a sixteenth-century Persian manuscript entitled *Bagh-I-Wafu*. Legend recorded that Babur was the emperor who first brought the rose to India.

Babur's son, Humayun, lost the throne to Sher Shah Suri, a Pashtun ruler of India. Suri is remembered as a reformer who built the Grand Trunk Road, which helped unite distant countries. Bickering among Suri's successors set the stage for Humayun's return, although it took him twelve years to regain his father's thrown. A mere six months after succeeding, Humayun died.

Islam's Golden Age

Historians credit Humayun's son Akbar as the greatest of the Mughal emperors. Ruling from 1556 to 1605, he brought stability to the region. He introduced various social and judicial reforms and allowed freedom of religion among his subjects. He even tried to develop a new religion, Din-i-Ilahi, to replace both Hinduism and Islam, but it remained unaccepted.

Akbar made Lahore the region's capital. He brought scholars, traders, and other learned people there and formed a center of scholarship.

After Akbar's death, his son Jehangir, who reigned from 1605 to 1627, followed his father's reforms. As a result, Indian and Islamic culture flourished. Literature and the arts thrived. It appeared as if the endless changes in government were ending, and the entire region could prosper. Shah Jahan, who followed

Built in the sixteenth and seventeenth centuries, the tomb of Akbar is one of India's finest examples of architecture, as well as a unique blend of Islamic and Hindu styles. Akbar, crowned in 1556 at the age of fourteen years after the death of his father, commissioned the tomb before his own death in 1605. The structure was completed by his son Jahangir. Four gardens beyond the gateway (pictured here) led to the pyramidal tomb inside. The structure itself features Persian-styled calligraphy and majestic marble minarets.

Jehangir's reign from 1628 to 1658, is best known for having the opulent Taj Mahal constructed.

Under Babur and his successors, Persian and Turkish cultural influences mingled with local culture, leading to new developments. One was the emergence of Sikhism, a religion that derives from Islam and Hinduism. Spread by Guru Nanak, a villager from Punjab influenced by Muslim and Hindu mystical traditions, Sikhism combined the Muslim belief in monotheism with the Hindu belief in reincarnation. A new language, Urdu, evolved out of a mixture of Persian and Indian dialects. The word "Urdu" means "camp" or "tent," and the name indicates that the language first evolved where soldiers from different regions interacted.

Shah Jahan was imprisoned by his son, Aurangzeb, in 1658 and died soon after. Historians are divided over Aurangzeb's legacy. Some see him as the last great Mughal emperor, who desperately tried to unite the empire in the face of continuous uprisings. Other historians note Aurangzeb's puritanical lifestyle and religious bigotry, which alienated popular support. He applied strict interpretations of Islamic law that imposed extra taxes on non-Muslims. Aurangzeb dealt with uprisings, many of them organized along religious lines, with a firm hand. In the north, the Sikhs were organized by Gobind Singh, their last guru, into a Khalsa "pure" brotherhood, and in the west, the Marathas were led by Shivaji. Both were seeking independence from Mughal rule.

The legendary Taj Mahal (*above*), near Delhi, India, is a magnificent example of Islamic architecture and the glory of Mughal achievement. Nadir Shah (*left*), shah of Persia (Iran) from 1736 to 1747, is considered the last of the greatest Asian conquerors. He is remembered for sacking Delhi and Lahore, stealing treasures, and extending the Persian Empire to its greatest height since the time of the Sassanids.

Aurangzeb inherited an empire that was already overextended. He faced rebellious provinces, and most of his reign was spent rushing from one region to another, quelling revolts. After his death in 1707, Nadir Shah, an Afghan, plundered Delhi and stole the famed Peacock Throne, securing it for the shahs of Iran.

Later, another Afghan, Ahmad Shah Abdali, seized control of north-western India and the Indus region, while the British were increasing their influence in the west around Calcutta.

THE BRITISH

The English were not the first Europeans to express interest in foreign trading in the East. Vasco da Gama, a Portuguese mariner, had discovered trade routes to India in 1498, and the Dutch followed.

In the late seventeenth century, Queen Elizabeth I granted a trading monopoly in the East Indies, later forming the East India Company. Asia's spices were greatly desired by Europeans, and the English wished to gain direct access to Indian markets.

During Jehangir's rule fifty years earlier, the English had arrived and begun trading. In time they became the dominant Europeans in the area. They established the strongest military force in the region, besetting the French, Dutch, and Portuguese.

The English were also laying claim to land and becoming forceful. Unlike the Arab influence, which arrived slowly, English influence immediately seeped into the culture. By the time the Mughals' rule weakened, they were poised to take over.

The East India Company

With their highly organized training, English forces were unmatched, and by 1686, they had won a number of battles against Mughal governors. In 1757, the Mughals lost the Battle of Plassey to Robert Clive, the governor of the English trading post in Madras and then in Calcutta from 1764 to 1767. The victory clearly established England's superiority in the region.

After the victory, the English proceeded with a strategy of signing "treaties" with local rulers, allowing them to keep their thrones while granting the British control over the military and the collection of revenue. Only on rare occasions would the British conquer a state and establish their own government. Using these tactics, the East India Company had control over most of India in the 1800s, although they allowed the Mughal emperor in Delhi to remain partially empowered. After allegations of corruption, the British appointed governor-generals to oversee the company's affairs.

In 1799, Lahore's seat was passed on to Ranjit Singh, a Sikh chief. The nineteen-year-old Singh spent the next three decades turning Lahore into a formidable force. By the time of his death in 1839, the Sikhs were rulers of the entire Punjab region, including Kashmir, Ladakh, Baltistan, Gilgit, Hazara, and the Peshawar Valley.

The British recognized Singh's successes and struck a treaty with him in 1809, with Singh promising to leave British territory alone. After his death, however, his successors ignored the treaty, which led to two

British imperialism reached new heights in the eighteenth century as seen in this map (right). Robert Clive, a British East India Company soldier, defeated a provincial Indian ruler in the Battle of Plassey (left) in 1757. This victory enabled the British to dominate India. In his 1772 speech to the British House of Commons, Clive called India "a paradise [that] abounds in very curious and valuable manufactures, sufficient not only for its own use, but for the use of the whole globe." Vasco da Gama (above) was the first European to establish a sea route to India in 1498.

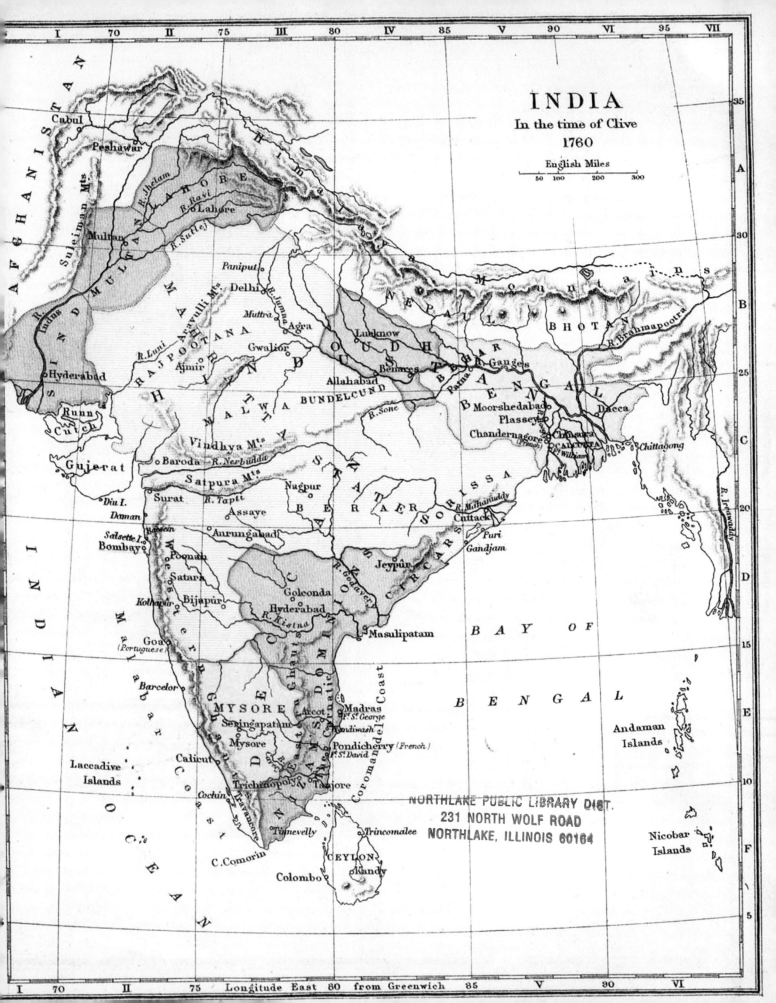

INDIA
In the time of Clive
1760

English Miles

50   100   200   300

violent confrontations between Indian and British forces in 1846. The Punjab region was now under British rule.

Part of the territory that Ranjit Singh had conquered included present-day Kashmir. The British sold the territory to Gulab Singh, the Hindu prince of Jammu, for $750,000. This provided the British with a friendly ally who separated them from the Russian invaders who came into the Indian region from the north. But it also installed a Hindu king over a region inhabited by Muslims. This action would have grave consequences later at the time of independence (1947).

Meanwhile, the British also influenced neighboring Afghan lands. At the time of Ranjit Singh's death in 1839, they occupied Kabul, Afghanistan. They returned King Shah Shuja, previously exiled by his own people, to the throne. He remained unpopular, which led to an uprising two

The Sikh Maharaja Gulab Singh of Jammu, founder of the last ruling house of Kashmir, is featured on this 1835 painting now housed in India's National Museum in New Delhi. To this day, Jammu and Kashmir remain disputed territories mostly inhabited by Muslims but claimed by both India and Pakistan.

years later. The battle was vicious and some 16,000 soldiers and citizens were killed.

The British Raj

The British grew arrogant and began ignoring treaties with Indian rulers. An example was the way they marched across Sindh to reach Afghanistan, annoying the various *amirs* (local leaders). When Sindh objected, the British forcibly added Sindh land to their holdings.

The local populace could take only so much abuse by their occupiers, and in 1857 there was an uprising. Called the Indian Mutiny by the British and the First War of Independence by the Indians, the area remained chaotic for nearly a year. The chaos marked the end of power for the East India Company, and a new viceroy was appointed to act on the Crown's behalf. Mughal rule formally ended, and the puppet emperor, Bahadur Shah, was exiled to Burma (present-day Myanmar).

With the British government now actively controlling India, it was free to exert its influence. Railroad tracks were laid, the English language replaced Persian and Urdu, and English laws and customs were introduced to the people. Although pockets of resistance remained, the Indian population soon accepted British rule. India, the richest British colony, was considered the jewel of the British Empire. The British held former Muslim rulers responsible for the revolt of 1857, and they were harsh on the Muslim ruling elite. By contrast, Hindus adopted English education and soon occupied positions in the British bureaucracy. Muslims, much slower to adapt to British rule, still considered themselves rightful leaders. This attitude cost them over time as Muslims remained uneducated and lacked influence with the British.

As part of their expansion, the British occupied Quetta in 1877. This led to an 1896 decision to create the province of Baluchistan.

New Borders and Provinces

During 1879, the British again tried to gain control of Afghanistan. They occupied Kabul, installed a man of their choosing on the throne, and repeated their 1839 attempt to gain central Asian territory.

Once again they failed; Sir Louis Cavagnari was murdered, and the English retreated. By 1893, the British and Afghanistan's Shah Abdur Rahman settled on a border at the Durand Line. Despite Afghan protest, the British divided the Pashtun homeland in half, angering those living in the Pashtun area. Within four years, there was an uprising that nearly beat British forces.

Platelaying - Darweza Quetta section of S. P. Ry

After the completion of this railway through Baluchistan in 1887 (top and bottom left) the rush was on to lay tracks north across the Peshin Plateau toward the North-West Frontier province, reminding the Russians that Britain wanted no interference in the region. Regimental plaques (top right) commemorate those troops that served periods of duty near the Khyber Pass in the North-West Frontier province.

In reaction, a 1901 agreement established the North-West Frontier province that centered the Pashtun land at its core. Similar to the Baluchistan decision a few years earlier, this agreement left a stretch of Pashtun land independent. Britain recognized that Indian citizens would never consent to foreign rulers.

However, locals continued to skirmish with British forces well into the late 1930s.

Searching for Independence

One result of British social reforms was the rise of an intellectual class. These people, most of them Hindu, often studied in England and

Europe, and returned to India with ideas of freedom, equality, and self-governance. In 1885, some of them formed the Indian National Congress with the aim of lobbying the British to allow Indian participation in government. Some Muslims, who felt that their community lagged behind the Hindus socially and economically, did not support the idea of self-governance. Leaders like Sir Syed Ahmad Khan argued that Muslims should concentrate on scientific education and remain loyal to British authorities.

The Congress, meanwhile, succeeded in getting the British to hold limited elections. This increased Indian participation, rapidly evolving their campaign into a movement for complete independence. Fearing that the Muslims would again be forgotten, a group of Muslim businessmen and rulers,

governing under the British, formed the All-India Muslim League in 1906.

The Muslim League was aimed at winning similar concessions—seats in legislative councils, membership in government bodies—as the Congress, but it remained loyal to the British. The League argued that since Muslims were a minority in British India (30 percent of the population), they needed special concessions to ensure they were not swamped by the Hindu majority.

Northern Areas

North-West Frontier Province

Punjab

Baluchistan

Sindh

ARABIAN SEA

The British-Settled Border of Pakistan, the Durand Line

- - - - - - - - -

Afghanistan attacked British holdings in 1919, but superior arms and air power decided the British victory. That same year, the British massacred protestors from the Amritsar region, which ignited a more militant approach to the goal of independence.

It was during this time that Mohandas Karamchand Gandhi rose to prominence. Using nonviolence and civil disobedience, he electrified the Indian people and bewildered the British.

At this time, a senior Muslim leader in the Congress, Muhammad Ali Jinnah, switched sides and joined the Muslim League. Jinnah tried to forge some unity with the Congress as witnessed in the Lucknow Pact of 1916. A turning point came in 1919 when the British defeated the Ottoman Empire and decided to abolish the position of caliph. For Muslims this was an emotional issue, and Gandhi used this to forge unity between Hindus and Muslims. Joint protests were organized, and Muslims joined Hindus in the first-ever mass rallies seen in the freedom struggle.

Muslim leaders continued to fight for beneficial changes in their way of life. Among these new demands was the separation of Sindh from Bombay and naming Baluchistan as a separate province. The All-India Muslim League agreed to address social issues with Sir John Simon and his Statutory Commission.

The commission first met in 1927 but was criticized by its lack of diverse attendants. A rival All-Parties Conference met instead, with Jawaharlal Nehru's committee. Despite well-intentioned attitudes, little was accomplished.

Mohandas Karamchand Gandhi, known as Mahatma, (1869–1948), was a pacifist Indian leader and reformer who sought to free India from the caste system and hailed Britain's decision to grant Indian independence as "the noblest act of the British nation." His last months were darkened by strife between Hindu and Muslim conflicts, but his fasts to shame instigators helped to avoid deeper tragedies. A Hindu fanatic assassinated Gandhi in Delhi on January 30, 1948.

Although Hindus and Muslims did come together under Gandhi, their unity was short-lived. Muslim leaders remained concerned that the Indian National Congress did not adequately represent the religious group. It was clear that once free, India would adopt the British parliamentary style government. This system would favor Hindus, who made up about 70 percent of the population. In order to safeguard Muslim interests, the Muslim League wanted separate electorates—each legislature to have a fixed number of seats for which only Muslims could vote. This would ensure that there was always a certain percentage of Muslims (in proportion to their population) in the legislature. The Congress repeatedly refused this demand, asserting that it was a secular (non-religious)

party and did not represent Hindu interests. The Congress felt that such a move would divide Indian society along religious lines.

This 1909 map of the island of Bombay, which lies off India's western shores, was originally printed in *The Gazetteer of Bombay City & Island*. A British holding since 1668, the natural trading post with a large harbor became independent with the rest of India in 1947 and was renamed Mumbai during the 1990s.

ISLAND OF BOMBAY

English Miles

5 | THE LAND OF THE PURE

CASPIAN SEA ——

PERSIAN GULF ——

After decades of negotiation, a proposal was put forth for a separate Muslim country in 1930. Dr. Allama Muhammad Iqbal, a Punjabi philosopher, suggested a separate Muslim state during his inaugural address as president of the All-India Muslim League. Most Muslim leaders favored this idea, while the Indian National Congress strongly opposed it.

A Separate Muslim State

Meanwhile, a Muslim student at England's Cambridge University, Chaudhri Rahmat Ali, made a similar call along with fellow expatriates in 1933. Ali named the land Pakistan, which means "Land of the Pure," in his pamphlet "Now or Never."

England had already hosted three conferences before 1932 to discuss India's fate. As

At the time of independence from British India (1947), Pakistan became the only country in the world that was divided into two parts with an entire nation between them. East Pakistan was home to Bengalis while West Pakistan was composed of individuals from several different provinces. In 1971, East Pakistan seceded and became known as Bangladesh (*right inset*). The name of the remaining western half of the country—Pakistan— is also an acronym for the origins of the people who live there, according to some, but most people believe that Pakistan's literal meaning is "Land of the Pure."

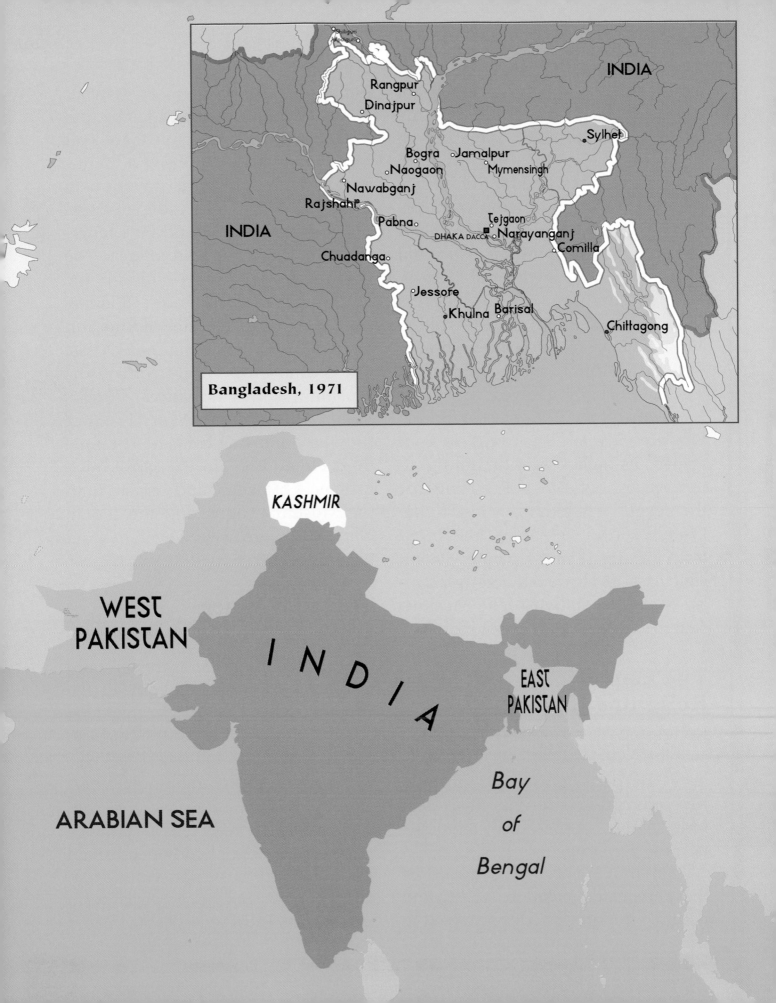

Bangladesh, 1971

Shiliguri
Jalpaiguri
Rangpur
Dinajpur
INDIA
Sylhet
Bogra   Jamalpur
Naogaon   Mymensingh
Nawabganj
Rajshahi
Pabna   Tejgaon
DHAKA DACCA   Narayanganj
INDIA   Comilla
Chuadanga
Jessore
Khulna   Barisal
Chittagong

KASHMIR

WEST
PAKISTAN

I N D I A

EAST
PAKISTAN

ARABIAN SEA

Bay
of
Bengal

expected, the Muslim and Hindu representatives disagreed on key issues. Muhammad Ali Jinnah revived the All-India Muslim League in time for the 1935 elections. Although it failed to win the majority of votes, it did diminish Muslim support for the Indian National Congress, led by Jawaharlal Nehru.

The Hindu-majority Congress spent the next several years recruiting Muslims to their cause, attempting to dull the Muslim League's influence.

Britain finally allowed provincial governments in 1940, elected by the whole population. The Congress continued its policy of attempting to remove any opposition. Realizing that the League would always lose to the Congress in joint elections, Jinnah put forth a demand for a separate Muslim state in 1940. He demanded the country be divided in two. Many Muslims saw this idea as the only solution.

The Gap of Religions Grows

Religious, not political, ideology swayed voters after the first elections. Tensions between Hindus and Muslims grew stronger. It wasn't long before verbal disagreements became physical.

The British were well aware of these repeated calls for a Muslim nation. Sir Stafford Cripps arrived in India in 1942 with plans to grant its independence. In response, he put forth his Cabinet Mission Plan. This idea called for three tiers of administration with a central government based in Delhi to handle defense. The subcontinent would be a federation of three separate states. The first section would contain the Hindu-majority provinces: Bombay (Mumbai), Madras, the Central and United Provinces, Bihar, and Orissa. The second third would contain the Muslim-majority provinces: Punjab, Sindh, the North-West Frontier province, and Baluchistan. The final third would contain the Muslim-led provinces of Bengal and Assam. Both the Muslim League and the Indian National Congress, however, rejected his proposals.

The Sikh Voice

Almost unseen during this struggle between the Hindu and Muslim populations was the rising voice of the Sikhs. Led by Tara Singh, they first called for their homeland, Punjab, to be independent from India. The Sikhs, who actually represented only 2 percent of the population, were disproportionately represented in Britain's armed forces. They had hoped Britain would reward that valor with a separate country, but their pleas were ignored. Instead Punjab, which had a sizable Muslim population also, was split between India and Pakistan.

Finally, a member of the Congress named Rajgopalacharia put forth a proposal for a land division that ultimately became the blueprint for separation talks in coming years.

During World War II, the Indian people were not directly involved in the fighting, though Indian soldiers were deployed. This allowed the Muslim separatist movement to gain momentum. As the war wound down, the current viceroy, Lord Wavell, held the 1945 Simla Conference in a failed attempt to resolve the matter.

After an April 1946 election, the All-India Muslim League held a convention at Delhi. Hussain Shaheed Suhrawardy, the chief minister of Bengal, again demanded a separate Muslim nation. The League declared August 16, 1946, as Direct Action Day to show Muslim solidarity (unity) around the country. While noble in its goals, it led to a bloody riot in Calcutta that left more than 4,000 people dead.

Progress toward self-rule and ultimate independence, stalled by World War II, continued. By then, the era of colonization by European powers was ending around the globe. It was just a matter of time before India would be free once more, although Muslims were openly questioning their position in independent India.

England, which had tried to mediate between the two groups, proposed a joint Indian government, but Jinnah rejected the plan. He refused to work under Nehru.

A New Country

In February 1947, Lord Louis Mountbatten was named the region's new viceroy, replacing

Master Tara Singh, 1885–1967, (*right, standing*) was an outspoken Sikh and Indian politician. Seen here speaking at a conference in 1943, he argued against the formation of a separate Muslim state (Pakistan) and met with then Muslim leader Muhammad Ali Jinnah, who appealed to him as well as other Sikhs in 1946. Later, Singh declared, "Death to Pakistan," from a dias in Lahore to a crowd of more than 50,000 who then began rioting. In the days and months that followed, thousands of Hindus, Muslims, and Sikhs were murdered both before and after Pakistan separated from British India.

Wavell. He immediately proclaimed that independence would finally occur in June 1948. He also acknowledged that a separate Muslim land was needed. His notion was to divide the Punjab and Bengal areas in half, hoping to remove the possibility of a civil war. Gandhi disliked the plan and wanted Mountbatten to invite Jinnah to govern a united India. Nehru, though, vetoed the notion.

Mountbatten set up elections that allowed various regions to determine their fates—joining either India or the proposed state of Pakistan. Areas with large concentrations of Hindus and Muslims ultimately elected divisions along religious concentrations. One such area was Bengal, though neither faith was satisfied. Sir Cyril Radcliffe was asked to settle this matter.

Mountbatten, after Britain's Parliament approved the Indian Independence Act in July, moved up the date of independence from June 1948 to August 1947.

This photograph was taken in Calcutta, India, on August 24, 1946, one year before India gained its independence from Britain. Eight days earlier, a huge crowd began gathering to attend the Muslim League Direct Action Day meeting in protest against British negotiations on India. Tensions were high between Hindus and Muslims, who turned on one another in acts of violent bloodshed over the Muslim demand for a separate state.

As the date neared, Radcliffe's new boundaries remained questionable. In fact, some twelve million people moved across the line dividing east and west Punjab. Some six million people fled from Hindu to Muslim land while the other half went in the opposite direction. It was not a smooth transition and resulted in countless acts of violence. No accurate records exist, but estimates of those left dead by the transfer of populations range between 200,000 and 1,000,000 casualties.

When everything was settled, a substantial number of Muslims remained in India, while a smaller number of Hindus chose to live in Pakistan.

What remained to be settled was the final fate of the numerous small "princely" states that had allegiance to the British Crown. Lord Mountbatten urged all annexed areas to align with India or Pakistan.

East and West Pakistan

Jinnah was Pakistan's first leader in the role of governor-general and the first person to begin coping with the results of the partition. Pakistan's lands held few natural resources. Pakistan was split in two, with 1,000 miles of Indian territory buffering the land. Baluchistan, Sindh, and Punjab lands lay to the west. To the east were parts of Bengal and Sylhet.

The east consisted of indigenous Sindhis, Punjabis, and Balochis, who had their own languages and culture, as well as Urdu-speaking migrants from the lands now belonging to India. West Pakistan, on the other hand, was entirely Bengali-speaking. Economically, East Pakistan consisted of landowners, professionals, and bureaucrats, while the west was less economically developed. This led to strained relations between the two regions, which many see as the result of the east's tendency to look down on the west.

Faith alone was not enough to support a divided country. Jinnah angered people on both sides by naming Urdu as the official state language. He also wanted Pakistan to be a secular state, meaning all religions could be tolerated, which angered some Muslims. After some thirteen months in office, Jinnah died. Liaquat Ali Khan became the next prime minister and began his rule in the midst of a war. He made an effort to bring the strict clerics to his side by proclaiming, "Sovereignty over the entire universe belongs to Allah Almighty alone."

Not surprisingly, Hindu members of the assembly protested the new leader's proclamation.

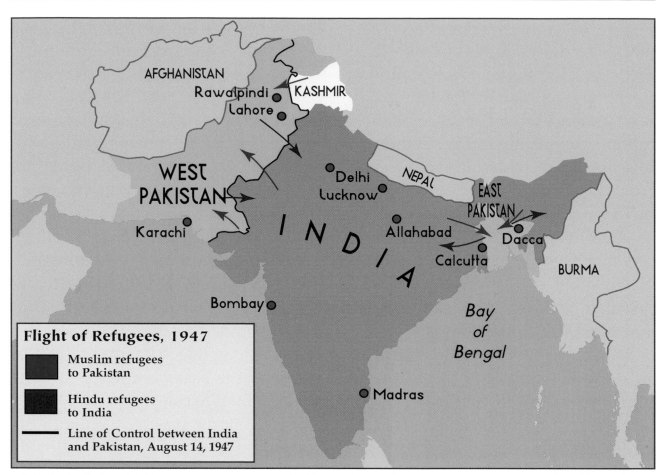

Flight of Refugees, 1947

■ Muslim refugees to Pakistan

■ Hindu refugees to India

— Line of Control between India and Pakistan, August 14, 1947

After India declared Pakistan a separate state, Baluchistan, the North-West Frontier province, and Sindh split from British India immediately, but the country still had the difficult task of dividing Bengal and Punjab. Afterward, more than seven million Muslims left India while a similar number of Hindus journeyed out of the newly created Pakistan. The migration of both peoples resulted in terrible bloodshed and bitterness. Although an exact number is difficult to estimate, some historians believe that as many as one million people could have died in the process.

Fighting for Kashmir

In October 1947, Pashtun Afridi warriors from Pakistan's North-West Frontier province declared *jihad* (holy war), believing Kashmir's Maharaja (fighting soldiers) were about to hand over the Muslim majority state to India. The Maharaja called upon India for help with the uprising, which more or less sealed Kasmhir's fate.

Nehru sent troops from India across the Line of Control to Kashmir, as did Pakistan, which ignited the first war between the two countries. The fighting stopped in January 1949 after a United Nations cease-fire was established. Kashmir was then divided, with Pakistan gaining control over Gilgit, Baltistan, and the western side of the Kashmir Valley, while India gained control of Jammu and Ladakh. A referendum, still pending, was promised to determine Kashmir's fate.

Muhammad Ali Jinnah

Muhammad Ali Jinnah was born December 25, 1875, the son of a successful businessman. He was trained at the Sindh Madrasa and then at Karachi Mission School. In 1892, he traveled to England to study law. By 1896, he qualified for the bar and was called to practice law a year later.

Attending the Indian National Congress as a secretary in 1906 propelled Jinnah into politics. In 1910, he was elected to the Imperial Legislative Council, where he grew close to Muslim leaders. By March 1913, Jinnah formally joined the All-India Muslim League with a goal of achieving Hindu-Muslim unity. This culminated in the annual sessions of the Congress and the League occurring at Lucknow at the same time in 1917. Joint proposals, known as the Lucknow Pact, were approved.

When the Nehru Report was issued in 1928, rejecting Muslim demands for separate elections, Jinnah's hopes for unity were dashed.

By 1934, he was elected president of the Muslim League, a title he held until his death. As Pakistan was born on August 14, 1947, Jinnah was there as its first governor-general. Pakistanis revere him as *Quaid-I-Azam*, or "Great Leader."

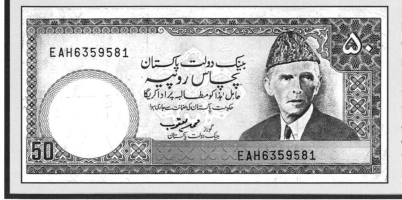

Muhammad Ali Jinnah (1875–1948), beloved leader of the Muslim League, whose slogan was "Islam in Danger," is shown here on Pakistani currency. He is most often remembered for submitting the Lahore Resolution (also known as the Pakistan Revolution, the first time an official demand was made for the creation of a Muslim state). Just one year after he became governor-general, however, he died of tuberculosis.

Ali Khan was assassinated in 1952, which propelled Pakistan into chaos. Khwaja Nazimuddin replaced him. Militant Muslims demanded a "purification" of Pakistani life in 1953, continuing to pepper Nazimuddin with demands based on their religious beliefs. Dissatisfied, Muslims rioted, prompting Governor-General Ghulam Muhammad to replace Nazimuddin with Muhammad Ali Bogra.

The Islamic Republic of Pakistan

It took until March 1956 for Pakistan to finalize a constitution, when it adopted the British parliamentary style of government. The nation's name at that time changed to the Islamic Republic of Pakistan. Bogra's administration was restructured, ushering in the strong-willed Major General Iskander Mirza as

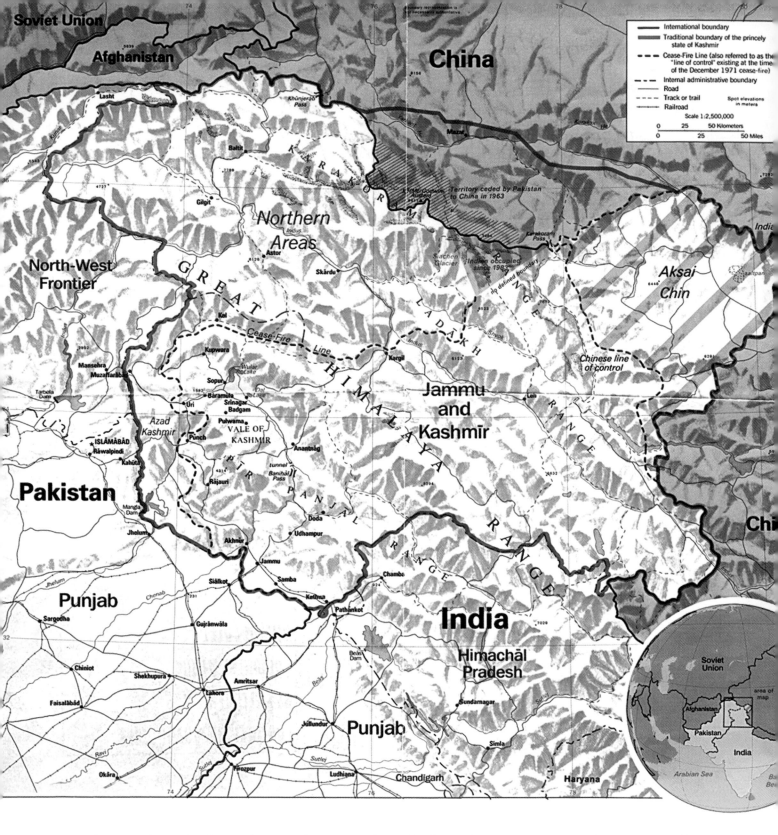

This map shows the disputed regions between India and Pakistan known as Jammu and Kashmir. The two mountainous areas have been sought after by Pakistan for years and at least five times have been the subject of small wars or near-war conflicts.

minister of the interior. But the new administration was unstable. Changes in administration were rapidly developing until Mirza stepped in as the country's new president. He wanted to stop the bickering between religious factions. It became so troublesome that on October 7, 1958, Mirza threw out the constitution and declared martial law.

Mirza appointed the army's leader, General Muhammad Ayub Khan, the new prime minister, but Mirza was soon after removed from office. Ayub Khan became the country's new president.

In 1959, Ayub Khan moved Pakistan's capital to Rawalpindi. Two years later, he began construction on a new capital in the city of Islamabad. Ayub Khan worked swiftly to transform his country, ratifying a new constitution in 1962. With aid from the United States and the World Bank, Pakistan was prospering, but differences between the west and east were rising.

Allies to the North

In 1962, China and India had a skirmish over territory in northern Kashmir that meant Pakistan had a powerful ally to the east. Two years later, China and India worked out a resolution that resolved a disputed Pakistan-China border at Karakoram. A road from Swat to Gilgit was expanded in 1966 and dubbed the "Friendship Highway."

Tensions over Kashmir mounted, igniting a battle in 1965. This conflict left Pakistan beaten and Ayub Khan alienated. He fired his foreign minister, Zulfiqar Ali Bhutto, in another wave of changes. By 1968, people were so angered by Ayub Khan's leadership that there was an attempt to assassinate him.

In March 1969, Ayub Khan resigned, turning the government over to General Agha Muhammed Yahya Khan. He immediately declared martial law and ended the self-rule of small city-states Chitral, Swat, Dir, Hunza, Nagar, and parts of Baltistan.

People could once again engage in political activities by the beginning of 1970, with general elections announced for December. Their outcome was affected when a cyclone ripped through East Pakistan, leaving much damage in its wake. The East Pakistanis were outraged by the lack of relief efforts from their countrymen in West Pakistan, increasing tension between the two sides.

6 BECOMING A NATION

Even though Zulfiqar Ali Bhutto, leader of the Pakistan People's Party, won a large percentage of the National Assembly seats in West Pakistan when elections were finally held in 1970, he actually lost. Sheikh Mujib and the Awami League took all of East Pakistan's seats, giving them a majority of votes. But Bhutto refused to participate in a government led by East Pakistan. General Agha Muhammed Yahya Khan was ineffective in forming a compromise and he was forced to suspend the entire assembly.

More Conflicts

In protest against West Pakistani chauvinism, East Pakistan went on strike. The army stepped in to restore order in March 1971, and Mujib was arrested, an act that set off a bloody civil war. One

The 1971 civil war over the states of Jammu and Kashmir resulted in the Simla Agreement of 1972, signed by both India and Pakistan. Though India still claims ownership of parts of both states and occupies areas of both, the Kashmiri people have been inspired to rise against Indian occupation of the mountainous region. Many have died in their fight as armies from both India and Pakistan continue to dominate the territory.

outcome was that some nine million people fled Pakistan to India, which in turn declared war on Pakistan. Once more the battle between the nations was brief, and Pakistan surrendered. India helped the Bangladeshi of East Pakistan form an independent state called Bangladesh.

By January 1971, Bangladesh was nearing independence, joining the British Commonwealth. Bhutto, in the meantime, replaced the ineffective Yahya as president of the smaller Pakistan. He had the country withdraw from the British Commonwealth, and it remained isolated until rejoining in 1990.

Bhutto acted swiftly to nationalize businesses, enact sweeping social reforms, and attempt a lasting peace through equality. In 1973, a new constitution was completed and the role of prime minister was restored. That February, Bhutto believed Baluchistan wanted to form its own

A 1971 photograph of Zulfiqar Ali Bhutto, then a foreign minister for Pakistan. In this image, taken at the United Nations in New York, Bhutto had just heard that the Indian government was willing to accept a cease-fire agreement in the Indo-Pakistani war after then U.S. United Nations ambassador George Bush introduced a resolution calling for peace in the region.

nation, so he fired its local government. This turn of events ignited new rioting that left 10,000 people dead.

Hoping to maintain the peace throughout the lower Asian continent, Bhutto met with India's prime minister, Indira Gandhi, daughter of the famed congressional leader Jawaharlal Nehru, in June 1972. At the meeting, the borders of Pakistan established in 1971 were confirmed, which more or less matched the 1949 divisions, but Pakistan maintained its claim on Kashmir. Still, tensions mounted again between the two countries. This uneasiness was intensified when India began secretly testing nuclear devices in 1974.

Pakistan Becomes a Dictatorship

After being accused of fraud in 1977, Bhutto resorted to martial law in several regions. The people seemed to have lost faith in the current government, which encouraged General Muhammed Zia ul-Haq to lead a coup on July 5. He extended martial law throughout the entire country and had Bhutto arrested. Bhutto was hanged for alleged crimes in April 1979.

Despite promising new general elections, Haq never carried them out and ruled as a dictator for more than seven years. Under his rule, strict Islamic laws replaced Bhutto's efforts to establish a secular government. At the same time, the Soviet Union invaded Afghanistan, which prompted the United States to fund military forces in Pakistan. This U.S. tactic, an extension of its Cold War policies, was aimed at halting any continued advance from the Soviets. It would also strengthen ties with Pakistan.

Haq welcomed refugees from Afghanistan and became a heroic leader in the world press. What didn't become apparent until later was that an unchecked flood of guns and illegal drugs were also crossing the border into Pakistan, which would later help to undermine its society. This would later fuel clashes between ethnic groups such as Pashtuns, Sindhis, and *muhajirs* (migrants).

China welcomed Haq in 1982, further bolstering his image as an appropriate leader for the country. He opened the northern areas and the Khunjerab Pass for traffic and

trade, eventually including tourism in 1986.

A Call for Democracy

Not everyone appreciated Haq's leadership, however, and from the ashes of previous political parties the Movement for the Restoration of Democracy started to form. Bhutto's widow, Nusrat, and daughter, Benazir, chaired his former party, the PPP. When they first attempted civil disobedience to rally support, Haq clamped down, forcing Benazir and others into exile. Still others died as a result of the protests.

Pressure mounted both internally and internationally for Pakistanis to have a greater say in their government. Haq finally allowed an election in February 1985 without the interference of any political parties. Martial law had finally ended.

Benazir spent her next few years in England, marrying Sindhi executive Asif Ali Zardari in December 1987. She spent most of her time speaking out on behalf of the Pakistani people and against Haq. Her words may have prompted Haq to dissolve the various state assemblies in May 1988, calling for new elections.

Haq and several of his staff died in a plane crash near Bahawalpur in Punjab on August 17. The cause of the crash has never been officially

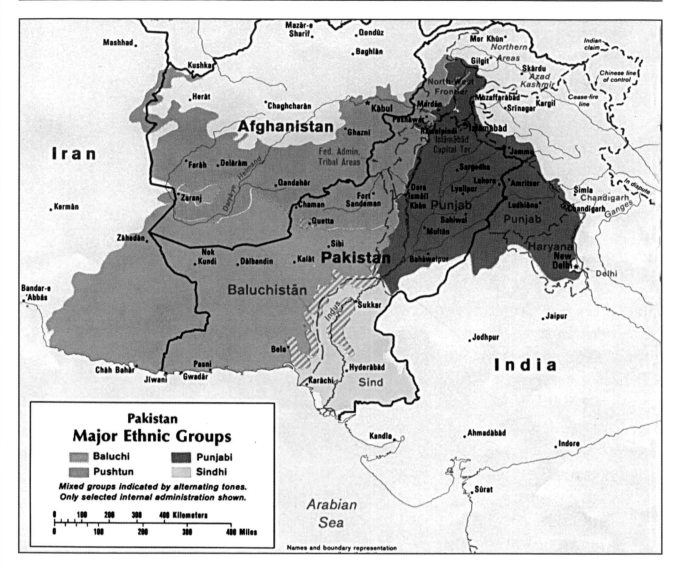

Pakistan
Major Ethnic Groups
- Baluchi
- Pushtun
- Punjabi
- Sindhi

Mixed groups indicated by alternating tones.
Only selected internal administration shown.

According to recent information provided by the U.S. Central Intelligence Agency (CIA), Pakistan's population is roughly 144,616,639. Among its varied ethnic groups are Punjabi, Sindhi, Pashtun (Pathan), Balochi, and *muhajir* (migrants from India at the time of the partition and their descendants).

documented. However, the president, Ghulam Ishaq Khan, took over until the next election in November, when the PPP won a majority vote and formed a coalition, or a temporarily aligned, government. Benazir returned to her homeland and, at thirty-five years of age, was sworn in as prime minister. She became the first woman to head a modern Muslim country.

Benazir Bhutto's tenure was far stormier than her father's, punctuated by a style that many Pakistanis considered arrogant. Her husband inflamed hard feelings with the constant threat of lawsuits against any media that was critical of his wife. Punjab's chief minister, Mian Nawaz Sharif, was her most outspoken critic. On the international stage, she had to deal with the ongoing conflict in Afghanistan as well as the testy relationship with India over Kashmir. Despite a July 1989 meeting with Rajiv Gandhi, India's prime minister, tensions remained high.

A Muslim-separatist movement gained strength in Indian-held Kashmir. The Indian army was sent to end the violence, leading to more bloodshed and protests.

President Ghulam Ishaq Khan, invoking the eighth amendment of the constitution, finally dismissed Bhutto's government on August 6, 1990. Her husband was arrested on charges of corruption. Ishaq Khan called for new elections in October, and Mian Nawaz Sharif became the new prime minister.

The United States and China

Nawaz Sharif hoped to stabilize the government and restore some sense of its order, but was dealt a harsh blow. The United States suspended all economic and military aid to Pakistan. The reason given was Pakistan's fledgling nuclear program, begun in 1975 as a response to India's nuclear testing.

The Gulf War prompted Pakistan to finalize a deal with China in 1991, which allowed the Chinese to assist Pakistan with the development of a nuclear power plant.

In 1992, the worst monsoon rains in a century pounded Pakistan. International relief efforts were mostly inadequate, and more than a million citizens were left homeless. Ishaq Khan was accused of slow and ineffectual leadership during Pakistan's recovery process. In fact, he made a pilgrimage to Mecca during the disaster, providing fuel to his critics.

Tensions rose between Ishaq Khan and Nawaz Sharif over the prime minister's actions. The government was further rocked when it became public knowledge that the military illegally influenced the outcome of various local elections.

As he did with Bhutto, Ishaq Khan used the constitution's eighth amendment to dissolve Nawaz Sharif's government in March 1993. Sharif turned to the country's supreme court to gain an order to maintain the current government, plunging the country into chaos. Fearing another military takeover, Ishaq Khan and Sharif resigned their posts, hoping this would quiet the people.

New elections were finally held by October and the PPP regained power, restoring Benazir Bhutto to the role of prime minister. Bhutto's administration faced more difficulties during its second tenure. She had to contend with rising religious conflicts within Muslim populations, especially Shiite-Sunni violence. Drug traffic into Pakistan also led to increased crime.

President Farooq Leghari almost immediately lost faith in his prime minister despite her efforts. It was a difficult position for anyone,

Benazir Bhutto, a representative of the Pakistan People's Party (PPP), was elected to the office of prime minister in 1988. In spite of the public's approval of her leadership, President Ghulam Ishaq Khan ousted her in a coup twenty months later in 1990. She was reelected in 1993 and served three consecutive years.

attempting to soothe a government that had again spiraled out of control.

The Rise of Extremist Groups

During the next few years, Pakistan became the scene of numerous skirmishes in nearly every region of the country. Death was becoming frighteningly commonplace on city streets. By September 1996, Murtaza Bhutto, Benazir's brother and outspoken critic, was shot to death, and Benazir was accused of sanctioning the attack.

At roughly the same time, the Pakistani army funded a fundamentalist group known as the Taliban that had gained power in Afghanistan. This was meant to cement ties between the two countries, but as the Taliban introduced strict Islamic law to the war-torn land, Pakistan was left as a bystander. The military continued to back terrorist groups that usually adhered to one strict fundamentalist interpretation of Islam.

Complicating matters was Bhutto's husband Zardari's corrupt financial dealings. His abuses also included using government money to fund a lavish lifestyle that was far out of the reach for the majority of Pakistanis. The couple seemed profoundly out of touch with the needs of the common people. President Leghari had little choice but to again dismiss Bhutto on November 5, 1996.

7 A COUNTRY DIVIDED

New elections were held in Pakistan in February 1997, and Nawaz Sharif found himself back in power. His All-India Muslim League had a majority in the lowest turnout for a Pakistani election. Once his party was installed in the National Assembly, they unanimously voted to repeal the eighth amendment of the constitution, ending the president's power to dismiss the prime minister.

Tensions over Kashmir escalated between Pakistan and India. India's administration became more volatile and resorted to more aggressive policies toward Pakistan, keeping the region destabilized.

Pakistan remained unstable as Sharif fought against the chief justice of the supreme court, Sajjid Ali Shah, over a variety of issues. Shah indicted Sharif on several charges, and Sharif rallied enough justices to vote Shah off the supreme court bench, which then prompted President Leghari to resign.

In May 1998, Pakistan tested its first nuclear devices in southwestern Baluchistan, responding to an earlier Indian nuclear test. Both countries were condemned by world governments for the action. Pakistan was hit especially hard by economic sanctions. One year later, threats of war broke out as fighting over Kashmir escalated.

General Pervez Musharraf assumed the role of prime minister during a bloodless coup in October 1999. Since he took power, Musharraf has attempted to

Pervez Musharraf

The New Delhi–born Pervez Musharraf was a member of one of the first families to migrate to Karachi in the newly founded Pakistan in 1947. His father was given an appointment in Turkey when Pervez was a youth, so he and his two brothers grew up in a foreign land. As an adult, he joined the army in 1964 and was awarded a medal for gallantry after the disastrous war against India in 1965. He rose through the ranks to a successful military career, resulting in his appointment as chief of the army forces in 1988. By April 9, 1999, he was named chairman of the Joint Chiefs of Staff Committee, which set the stage for his ability to structure a bloodless coup on October 12.

He continues to hold his military titles in addition to that of president, a title he added on June 20, 2001. American president George W. Bush turned to Musharraf for help in tracking down the terrorists responsible for the attacks against the United States on September 11, 2001. Musharraf saw an opportunity to promote his desire to end the influence of extremist groups and gain economic aid from the United States at the same time. Turning his back on the Taliban, a group his army helped empower, Musharraf became a staunch U.S. ally. Pakistan quickly became a staging ground for U.S. forces. Musharraf was elected to a seven-year term on April 30, 2002. His new term is complicated by tensions with India and internal criticism by some factions who dislike Pakistan's relations with the United States.

Pervez Musharraf first appointed himself chief executive of Pakistan's new dictatorial government in 1999, an act endorsed by most Pakistanis, but few Westerners.

end the influence of Islamic fundamentalists, who often provide personnel, arms, and money for terrorist operations. One year later, he named himself president.

India's Parliament was attacked by Muslim fundamentalists in December 2001. The Indian government accused the terrorists of being supported by Pakistan's government. Mirroring the United States's response to terrorism, India immediately mobilized its forces toward the Kashmir border. Pakistan pulled its troops from the Afghanistan border

This fortress railroad station in Lahore, Pakistan, is the only train station in the world that can be completely sealed by closing two gates. This function was not required until the Partition Crisis of 1947, ninety years after the station was built.

to meet the challenge. War seemed imminent, but despite the tension, it has not yet developed.

At stake is Kashmir, but those people living in the province have been continually agitating for their own independence. India has blamed Pakistan for funding the separatist movement, but as of 2002 had yet to furnish proof of any specific involvement.

Pakistan is now in the spotlight for its unwavering support of U.S. efforts to stop terrorists based in the Middle East. This, however, did not change the ongoing tensions with India over the fate of Kashmir. With both nations armed with nuclear weapons, the world is anxious over the potential of one country to act hastily. Musharraf has been outspoken about stabilizing Pakistan and no longer supporting extremist religious views. Pakistanis have supported his wishes, and with fresh funds, Musharraf has the ability to rebuild a fractured infrastructure.

His leadership will be tested, however, as he deals with the matter of Kashmir and Pakistan's ongoing relations with India.

TIMELINE

5000 BC Mesopotamia flourishes
3300 BC Writing begins in Sumer
2500 BC Egyptians build the Pyramids
2400 BC Assyrian Empire is established
2334 BC Rule of Sargon I
1750 BC Rule of Hammurabi in Babylonia
638 BC Approximate birth of Persian prophet Zoroaster (Zarathrustra)
600 BC Cyrus the Great establishes the Achaemenid Empire
563 BC Approximate birth of Buddha
331 BC Alexander the Great captures Babylon
323 BC Alexander the Great dies
AD 200 Sassanians rise to power
AD 226 Approximate date Zoroastrianism is reestablished under the Sassanids
AD 313 Christianity is accepted by the Romans
AD 570 Birth of Muhammad
AD 600 Roman, Parthian, and Kushan Empires flourish
AD 610 Muhammad's first revelation
AD 622 Buddhism begins its spread from India to Asia
AD 625 Muslims control Mesopotamia and Persia
AD 632 Death of Muhammad
AD 633–700 Followers of Islam start to spread their faith
AD 685 Shiite revolt in Iraq
AD 750 Abbasid caliphate begins in Iraq
AD 751 Arabs learn papermaking from the Chinese
AD 762 City of Baghdad is founded
AD 1215 Genghis Khan captures China and moves westward
AD 1220 Mongols sack Bukhara, Samarkand, and Tashkent
AD 1258 Mongols sack Baghdad
AD 1379 Timur invades Iraq
AD 1387 Timur conquers Persia
AD 1453 Ottoman Empire captures Constantinople and begins overtaking Asia
AD 1498 Vasco da Gama reaches India
AD 1526 Babur establishes Mughal Empire
AD 1534 Ottomans seize Iraq
AD 1554 First Russian invasion into central Asia
AD 1632 Taj Mahal is built
AD 1739 Nadir Shah invades the Mughal Empire, sacks Delhi
AD 1740 Ahmad Shah Durrani founds kingdom in Afghanistan
AD 1858 British rule is established in India
AD 1932 Saudi Arabia is founded by 'Abd al-'Aziz Al Sa'ud
AD 1947 Britain declares India's independence; East/West Pakistan succession
AD 1971 East Pakistan becomes Bangladesh
AD 1998 Pakistan tests its first nuclear device
AD 2001 Musharraf becomes Pakistan's president
AD 2002 Fighting on the border of Jammu-Kashmir region continues

GLOSSARY

amir A local leader, usually of a tribe.

caste system This system, which grouped people in strict socio-economic divisions, was developed in the Gangetic Valley and spread throughout India. Once born into a caste system, one was expected never to rise or fall in social class or occupation.

Cold War A condition of rivalry and mistrust between the United States and the Soviet Union in the mid- to late twentieth century.

coup (coup d'état) A French term meaning "blow to the state" that refers to a sudden, unexpected overthrow of a government by outsiders.

dictatorship A form of government in which absolute power is concentrated in one dictator, or in a small group.

exile To banish from one's country or home.

fundamentalism A movement or attitude stressing strict and literal adherence to a set of basic religious principles.

Harappan Name of an ancient civilization and one of the earliest known languages on Earth. Harappan eludes translation to this day. Also known as Mohenjodaran.

Hinduism The dominant religion of India. Hinduism emphasizes *dharma* (duty), with its resulting ritual and social observances.

Islam The religious faith of Muslims, including belief in Allah as the sole deity, and in Muhammad as his prophet.

khan A title denoting leadership or royalty, especially in central Asia.

Line of Control The Kashmir border separating India from Pakistan.

martial law Laws applied by military force during an occupation of any certain territory.

monotheism The belief in one god.

Muslim Someone who practices Islam.

partition A term used for the division of Asian land into India and Pakistan in August 1947.

Pashtun A collection of fiercely independent tribes on both sides of the Pakistan-Afghanistan border.

Sanskrit An ancient language of northern India.

Sikhism A blended religion featuring the Muslim belief in a single god and the Hindu belief in reincarnation.

United Nations An international organization formed after World War II to promote peace between nations.

Urdu A language culled from Persian and local Indian dialects; currently the national language of Pakistan.

viceroy A British term for governor of a territory.

FOR MORE INFORMATION

Asia Society and Museum
725 Park Avenue at 70th Street
New York, NY 10021
(212) 288-6400
Web site: http://www.asiasociety.org

Association for Asian Studies
1021 East Huron Street
Ann Arbor, MI 48104
(734) 665-2490
e-mail: jwilson@aasianst.org
Web site: http://www.aasianst.org

Silk Road Foundation
P.O. Box 2275

Saratoga, CA 95070
e-mail: info@silk-road.com
Web site http://www.silk-road.com/
    toc/index.html

Web Sites

Due to the changing nature of Internet
links, the Rosen Publishing Group, Inc.,
has developed an online list of Web
sites related to the subject of this book.
This site is updated regularly. Please
use this link to access the list:

http://www.rosenlinks.com/liha/paki/

FOR FURTHER READING

Caldwell, John C. *Pakistan* (Major
    World Nations). Broomall, PA:
    Chelsea House, 2000.
Crompton, Samuel Willard. *Pakistan*
    (Modern World Nations). Broomall,
    PA: Chelsea House, 2002.
Halliday, Tony. *Insight Guide: Pakistan.*
    Maspeth, NY: Langenscheidt
    Publishers, Inc., 2000.

Kenover, Jonathan Mark. *Ancient
    Cities of the Indus Valley
    Civilization.* New York: Oxford
    University Press, 1998.
King, John S. *Pakistan.* Oakland, CA:
    Lonely Planet Publications, 1998.
Wagner, Heather Lehr. *India and
    Pakistan* (People at Odds).
    Broomall, PA: Chelsea House, 2002.

BIBLIOGRAPHY

Farah, Mounir A., et al. *Global Insights
    People and Cultures.* New York:
    Macmillan/McGraw-Hill, 1994.
Halliday, Tony. *Insight Guide: Pakistan.*
    Masbeth, NY: Langenscheidt
    Publishers, Inc., 2000.
Islamic Republic of Pakistan. "History."
    Retrieved January 21, 2002
    (http://www.pak.gov.pk/public/
    govt/history.html).
King, John S. *Pakistan.* Oakland, CA:
    Lonely Planet Publications, 1998.
Lonely Planet World Guide. "Pakistan."
    Retrieved January 21, 2002

(http://www.lonelyplanet.com/
    destinations/indian_subcontinent/
    pakistan/history.htm).
Pakistan Information.com. "Pakistan."
    Retrieved January 21, 2002
    (http://www.pakistaninforma-
    tion.com/historyindex.html).
Quereshi, Rashid. "History of Pakistan."
    1998. Retrieved January 21, 2002
    (http://www.unigroup.
    com/PTIC/body_history.html).
Story of Pakistan. Retrieved January 21,
    2002 (http://www.storyofpakistan.
    com/default.asp).